Survival!

Animal Adaptations

By Alice Cary

Series Literacy Consultant
Dr Ros Fisher

Pearson Education Limited
Edinburgh Gate
Harlow
Essex CM20 2JE
England

www.longman.co.uk

ISBN 0 582 84132 1

Colour reproduction by Colourscan, Singapore
Printed and bound in China by Leo Paper Products Ltd.

The Publisher's policy is to use paper manufactured from sustainable forests.

10 9 8 7 6 5 4 3 2

The following people from **DK** have
contributed to the development of this product:

Art Director Rachael Foster

Martin Wilson **Managing Art Editor**	**Managing Editor** Marie Greenwood
Jane Tetzlaff **Design**	**Editorial** Jennie Morris
Helen McFarland **Picture Research**	**Production** Gordana Simakovic
Richard Czapnik, Andy Smith **Cover Design**	**DTP** David McDonald

Consultant David Burnie

Dorling Kindersley would like to thank: Shirley Cachia and Rose Horridge in the DK Picture Library; Lucy Heaver for additional research;
Johnny Pau for additional cover design work; and Jacqui Swan for additional design work.

Picture Credits: Alamy Images: Jan Baks 30cbr; Robert E. Barber 16cbr; Winston Fraser 9car; Gondwana Photo Art 10tr;
Mark Newman 14tl; James D. Watt 8cl. Ardea London Ltd: David Avon 4crb; Yann Arthus Bertrand 22–23; B. & P. Boyle 29tr. Nature Picture Library:
Anup Shah 30bl. Corbis: Jonathan Blair 22tl; Brandon D. Cole 21cbl; Darrell Gulin 13t; Dan Guravich 16t; Buddy Mays 1; Jose Fuste Raga 9b.
DK Images: Natural History Museum 7cfl; Parc Zoologique de Paris 5b. The Art Archive: 6–7. FLPA – Images of Nature: Minden Pictures 17cra.
Nature Picture Library Ltd: Terry Andrewartha 14–15. N.H.P.A.: ANT Photo Library 12b. Oxford Scientific Films: Chris Sharp 22t; Tom Ulrich 25tr.
Premaphotos Wildlife: 26b; Ken Preston-Mafham 28tl. Science Photo Library: Art Wolfe 17b; Ken M. Johns 29b. Getty Images: Kathy Bushue 13b;
John Giustina 25b; G.K. & Vicky Hart 12t; Jeff Hunter 21tr; Frans Lemmens 10–11b; Nacivet 3r; Paul Souders 20–21. Cover: Nature Picture Library:
David Curl front t. Still Pictures: Fred Bruemmer front bl.

All other images: © Dorling Kindersley © 2004. For further information see www.dkimages.com
Dorling Kindersley Ltd., 80 Strand, London WC2R 0RL

Contents

How Adaptation Works

An **adaptation** is a feature or way of behaving that makes a plant or an animal more likely to survive. In every **species**, some animals are better at surviving than others. These animals live long enough to mate, have babies and pass on their genes.

Adaptation does not occur during one animal's lifetime. It is a long, slow process that happens over many generations. However, the results of adaptation can be seen in individual animals.

A toucan's colourful and lightweight beak is specially adapted for grasping fruit from the branches of rainforest trees.

A crossbill's crossed beak is adapted for skilfully removing seeds from pine cones.

Animals that do not adapt to their environment often face **extinction**. This occurs when all the members of a particular species die out. A species can escape extinction by adapting to its environment. If the environment changes, then the animals that live there must change, too.

Most species of animals alive today have changed over a long period of time. In many cases, this change has been caused by some type of adaptation. Many of these animals have adapted so much that they look very different from their ancestors.

Classification

Living things are divided into large groups called kingdoms. All plants belong to the plant kingdom, while all animals belong to the animal kingdom. For example, people and rodents both belong to the animal kingdom. The large groups are then divided into smaller and smaller groups, ending with individual species. Humans are made up of a single species, but rodents are made up of about 1,700 different species.

If you compare the elephants of today with their distant ancestors, you can see how much they have changed.

The story of the peppered moth is a good example of how **adaptation** works. Some peppered moths have light-coloured wings, while others have dark-coloured wings.

During the mid-1800s, near Manchester, there were many more light-coloured moths than dark ones. Light-coloured moths blended in with the pale tree bark in their surroundings and the birds that ate them couldn't see them well. However, dark-coloured moths stood out clearly, so the birds ate them up. Soon there were only a few dark-coloured moths.

Manchester's smoky factories polluted the air and covered the trees with soot.

Then, in the 1850s, coal-burning factories sprang up all over Manchester. They produced dark smoke that covered trees with soot. Now light-coloured moths were easier for predators to spot than dark-coloured ones.

As the dark-coloured moths blended in better with the sooty background, more of them survived. They passed on their dark-coloured **genes** to their offspring. After years, there were more dark-coloured peppered moths than light-coloured ones.

A light-coloured peppered moth is easy to see against this background. However, a dark-coloured peppered moth is almost invisible against the same background.

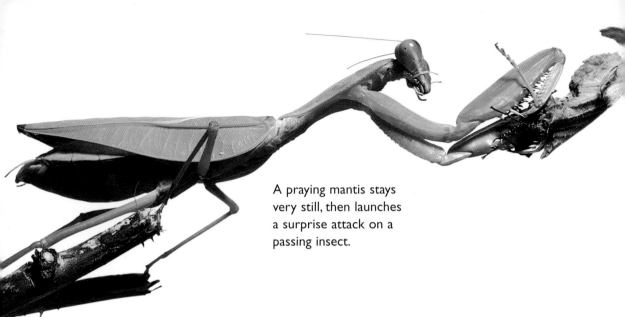

A praying mantis stays very still, then launches a surprise attack on a passing insect.

Great White Shark

The great white shark is well adapted to hunt in the ocean. It is a fast and powerful swimmer. It easily locates prey with its acute sense of smell. It can smell a single drop of blood in more than 100 litres of water.

Animals adapt in different ways. Sometimes the main colour pattern of the population changes. Sometimes the body size or shape changes. Sometimes an **adaptation** involves the way an animal behaves. This is known as **behavioural adaptation**.

For example, the praying mantis stays very still while waiting for a smaller insect to approach. This adaptation results in better hunters, which are more likely to survive.

Animals adapt in ways that help them to survive in their habitat. There are many different habitats in the world. This book looks at a few animals and the adaptations that help them to survive in their habitats.

Adaptation in the Desert:
Arabian Camel

The Arabian camel lives in herds in the deserts of Africa, Asia and central Australia. A desert is a place that gets less than 25 centimetres of rain each year. Deserts are often dry, sandy and windy. They are usually hot during the day and chilly at night.

The camel has adapted well to desert conditions. Its thick fur shields its skin from sunburn from the fierce desert Sun. The camel's fur also keeps it warm during the cool desert nights.

Desert Plants

Desert plants have also adapted to the extreme temperature of their environment. Cacti, for example, often have few or no leaves. This means that they lose very little water through their leaves. They also store water in their stems and have waxy skin to seal in moisture.

Arabian camel in the desert

The camel has several adaptations that allow it to hold moisture in its body. For example, a camel doesn't pant when it is hot. Therefore, it doesn't lose moisture in the form of saliva. Its nose also holds in moisture from the air as it breathes out.

A camel gets most of its water from the plants it eats. It has sharp teeth for cutting through the thick, thorny stems of desert plants. The tough lining of its mouth allows it to chew these prickly plants without harm.

A camel's strong teeth help it to cut through tough desert plants.

Some desert people use camels to carry things.

When a camel does find water, it drinks huge amounts at one time. A large camel can drink as much as 115 litres in 10 minutes. It can store the water for a few days.

Sand is quite difficult to walk on, but a camel has no trouble with it. A camel's foot has two toes that are far apart. A broad pad connects the toes. When a camel walks, this pad spreads out and keeps its feet from slipping or sinking into the sand.

Camel Humps

camel with full hump

camel with shrunken hump

When a camel goes a long time without eating, its hump shrinks and may even fall over to one side.

A camel also has several features that protect it from sandstorms. Thick fur lines the camel's ears and keeps sand out. A camel can also close its nostrils to the blowing sand. Three eyelids protect a camel's eyes. On the outer two eyelids, a double row of long eyelashes shields the eye. The inner eyelid is thin and transparent. It keeps dust from getting into a camel's eye.

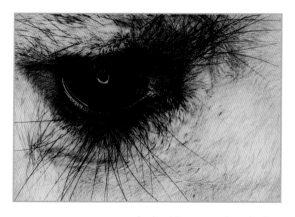

A double row of eyelashes helps to keep dust and sand out of a camel's eyes.

A camel also has a **behavioural adaptation** that stops it from getting too hot. A camel's body temperature is often lower than that of the surrounding air, so a group of camels can keep cool by leaning against one another.

These **adaptations** have developed over millions of years. They make a hot, dry habitat a camel's perfect home.

Australian Burrowing Frog

The Australian burrowing frog is another animal that is adapted to life in a hot desert. It survives a dry season by digging a hole in the ground and staying there for months until it rains. A layer of dead skin helps to keep the frog from drying out.

Adaptation in the Arctic:
Polar Bear

The polar bear lives in the Arctic, which has a cold, dry climate. Temperatures in the Arctic dip as low as minus 68°C.

A polar bear has two layers of thick fur. The top layer is made up of stiff, shiny hairs. These hairs look white, but they are actually clear. They let sunlight reach the second layer of fur, which is thick and woolly. This second layer of fur gathers heat from the sunlight and holds it in to keep the bear warm. In addition, a layer of blubber (or fat) under the bear's skin helps to keep heat in and cold out. Blubber can be more than 10 centimetres thick.

The Tundra

Some of the Arctic is made up of tundra – treeless plains.

Both the land and the ocean of the tundra region are in the polar circle. For most of the year, the average monthly temperature is well below freezing. The permanently frozen subsoil of this area is called permafrost.

polar bears on Arctic ice

A polar bear's nostrils close when it is underwater.

Sometimes even a polar bear can become *too* warm. To prevent overheating, it moves slowly and often stops to rest. Sometimes it will dive into the sea to cool off. A polar bear is a strong swimmer, which is important because it allows the bear to catch food in the water. A polar bear can swim for hours at a time, using its slightly webbed front paws like paddles. It holds its legs and back feet out flat and uses them like rudders for steering. It swims at up to 10 kilometres per hour.

A polar bear's large paws also help it
to walk over snow and ice. The paws can
be up to 30 centimetres wide. Its thick claws
help to keep it from sliding on the smooth
ice. Small, soft bumps on the thick pads of
the bear's feet also help it to grip the
ice and snow.

The polar bear is
the biggest and fiercest
hunter of the far north.

Polar bears can smell animals like these harp seals from more than 30 kilometres away.

A polar bear eats mainly seal meat. The polar bear is a good hunter. In winter, it finds a seal's breathing hole in the ice and waits patiently for a seal to come up for air. When a seal appears, the polar bear grabs the seal with its sharp claws and pulls it out of the water.

Successful **adaptations** mean that if there are no major climate changes in the Arctic, polar bears will thrive in this cold habitat for years to come.

Arctic Hare

Like the polar bear, the Arctic hare is well adapted to its habitat. Its thick winter coat provides warmth and helps it to blend in with the snow. It also has short ears, which reduce the amount of heat its body loses.

Adaptation in the Rainforest:
Three-toed Sloth

Tropical rainforests are warm and wet throughout the year. Most rainforests are found near the equator, where the Sun's rays hit Earth most strongly. During most of the year rain falls nearly every day, so plants and trees grow quickly.

Many different types of animals live in the different parts of the rainforest. Some creatures live in the tops of the tallest trees. Others are found in the branches and leaves of the canopy layer or on the rainforest floor.

a sloth in the rainforest

Rainforest Layers

Millions of animal and plant **species** live in the four layers that make up a rainforest:
- the forest floor
- the understorey
- the canopy
- the emergent layer.

Many rainforest animals live in the canopy. The canopy contains so much food that some of the animals that live there never set foot on the forest floor.

In the canopies of the Central
and South American rainforests the
three-toed sloth spends most of its life
upside down. It clings to a branch with
its specially adapted, long curved claws.
Even the sloth's fur is adapted to the animal's
upside-down lifestyle. Its fur grows from its belly
towards its backbone, so that rainwater runs off
its body as it hangs by all four legs.

The sloth sleeps for about 15 hours a day.
When it does move, it moves very slowly. Its neck has
many bones that enable the sloth to turn its head in
almost every direction. As it hangs upside down, the
sloth can reach the leaves all around it without
moving the rest of its body.

Leaf-cutter Ants

Leaf-cutter ants live on or under the forest floor. Worker ants snip bits of leaves from plants using their large, jagged jaws. Then at the colony other ants chew these bits into a mash. Soon a fungus begins to grow on the leaves. This fungus is the ants' main food.

A three-toed sloth eats, moves, sleeps and even gives birth while hanging upside down.

Such a slow-moving creature could be an easy target for predators. However, a sloth is protected by its appearance. Its colour and shape help it to blend in with its environment. When the sloth is curled into a ball, it looks like a clump of dead leaves or the stump of a branch. Often its predators, such as jaguars and leopards, don't notice it.

As humans clear large sections of the rainforest for timber and farming, they destroy the homes of many forest animals. If the sloths' leafy habitat disappears, then sloths might not be able to adapt quickly enough to avoid **extinction**.

Behavioural Adaptation: Migration

The humpback whale lives in the icy waters of the Arctic Ocean and the seas around Antarctica. An adult whale has a thick layer of blubber to keep it warm, but young whales don't. Young whales can't survive the extreme cold, so mother whales travel to warmer waters near the equator to give birth.

This journey is thousands of kilometres long, and is called **migration**. Migration is a **behavioural adaptation**. When animals migrate, they move to a place that has better living conditions. For humpback whales, migration is necessary so their calves survive.

A humpback whale's long fins make it a good swimmer.

A baby humpback whale stays very close to its mother when it migrates.

Groups of humpback whales often herd fish towards the surface by blowing bubbles underwater.

Whale Song

One of the greatest mysteries of the animal kingdom is the whale song. In breeding waters, male humpback whales make a long series of calls, or a "song". These calls can last from 2 to 40 minutes.

Scientists don't know why the whales make these calls or what they mean. Some think it attracts females or wards off other males.

Whales from the same breeding group appear to sing the same song.

A tern parent feeds its chick.

Many birds migrate to stay warm or to find food. The Arctic tern travels twice a year to find food and warmer weather.

In summer the tern stays in the far north where it lays its eggs and raises its young. At the end of the summer the Arctic days get colder and shorter, and food becomes scarce. Then the tern flies south to Antarctica where summer is beginning and there is plenty of food. Towards the end of the Antarctic summer, the tern begins its long flight back to its Arctic breeding grounds. To make its yearly **migration** a tern flies 35,000 kilometres.

A wildebeest follows its instinct to migrate even when it means crossing dangerous rivers.

Many animals, such as the wildebeest, know that the time has come to migrate when cold weather approaches or when its food supplies dwindle. However, some migratory birds start their flight back from the tropics when there's still plenty of food.

Migration is a complicated **adaptation**. Scientists are still learning about how animals know when to migrate and how they find their way. They think that some animals may be guided by the Sun, the Moon and stars, while other animals use rivers and mountain ranges as signposts.

Monarch Butterfly

Each year millions of monarch butterflies fly up to 4,000 kilometres south from Canada and the United States to spend the winter in Mexico. In the spring they return to the north and lay their eggs on their way.

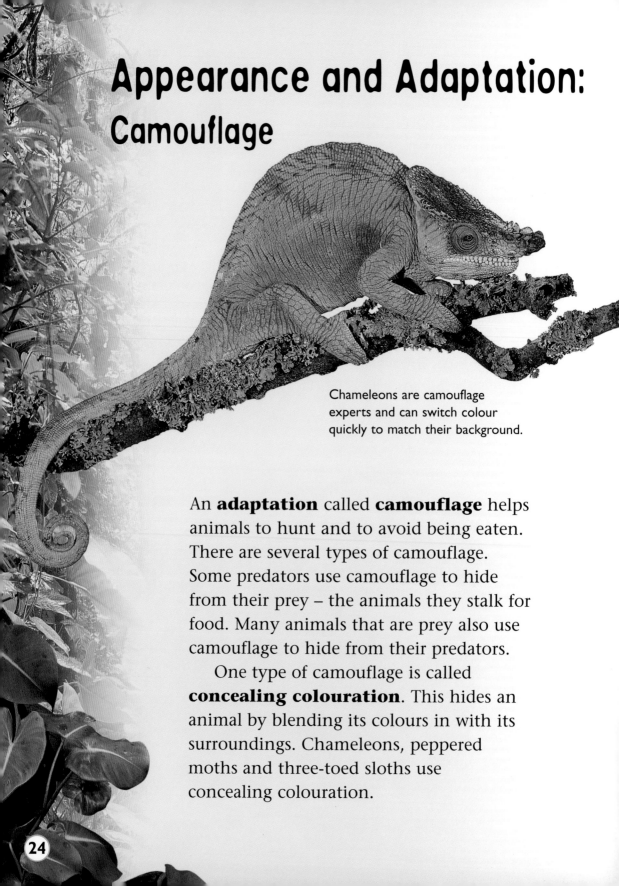

Appearance and Adaptation:
Camouflage

Chameleons are camouflage experts and can switch colour quickly to match their background.

An **adaptation** called **camouflage** helps animals to hunt and to avoid being eaten. There are several types of camouflage. Some predators use camouflage to hide from their prey – the animals they stalk for food. Many animals that are prey also use camouflage to hide from their predators.

One type of camouflage is called **concealing colouration**. This hides an animal by blending its colours in with its surroundings. Chameleons, peppered moths and three-toed sloths use concealing colouration.

Zebras in a herd use **disruptive colouration**. It is called *disruptive* because it disrupts – or breaks up – the outline of the animal. When zebras are together, all their stripes blend together so that one zebra can't be picked out for attack by a predator. This helps to keep the whole herd safe.

A fawn's spots let it blend in with the Sun-dappled forest floor.

As added protection, each zebra has special stripes that hide its eyes. Predators often focus on their prey's eyes in order to set that animal apart from all the rest. These eye stripes stop the predator from picking out one zebra from the herd.

Zebras' stripes help them to hide out in the open.

Disruptive colouration tricks predators. Some insects such as the banana eater butterfly in New Guinea have false "eyes" on their wings. These eyes distract a predator from its real eyes. Even if it loses a piece of its wing, the butterfly can still fly away.

The Australian hairstreak butterfly has another way of confusing its predators. The rear edges of its wings have dark markings, which look like a head. A predator often sees the false head first and attacks the wrong end of the butterfly.

A predator will attack the banana eater butterfly's fake "eyes" instead of its body.

The Australian hairstreak butterfly has a false head.

It is difficult to see a vine snake when it curls around leafy branches in a tree.

The flower mantis's colours match the flowers in which it hunts.

A vine snake looks like the part of the plant it clings to. This **disguise** often fools the frogs and lizards that are its prey, so it can pounce and surprise them.

An insect called the flower mantis has a disguise that makes it look like blossom. It even moves backwards and forwards, so that it looks as if it is being blown by the breeze. When an insect approaches the "flower", the mantis reaches out with its front legs and grabs it.

Can you tell the difference between a bee (right) and a harmless hoverfly (left)?

This grass snake has been threatened by a predator and is pretending to be dead.

A hoverfly uses **mimicry** to hide from its predators. This means that it looks like a different animal. It looks like a bee, but while the hoverfly is harmless, a bee has a sting. Predators that have been stung by a bee will not try to eat a hoverfly. Therefore, hoverflies that look most like bees are most likely to survive.

Some animals practise mimicry by pretending to be dead. When a grass snake is threatened by a predator, it rolls over on its back and pretends to be dead. Many predators will not eat dead animals, so this behaviour usually saves the snake.

Camouflage is an **adaptation** that helps predators and prey to survive. Prey that has good camouflage will not be seen by its predators. This allows it to live long enough to mate and have young. These young are likely to have similar colouring to their parents.

This is also true for a predator. If it has good camouflage, then it will surprise its prey. This will allow it to catch enough food to survive and live long enough to have young.

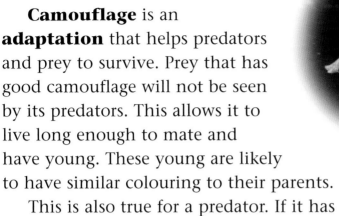

A leafy sea dragon looks like a clump of seaweed.

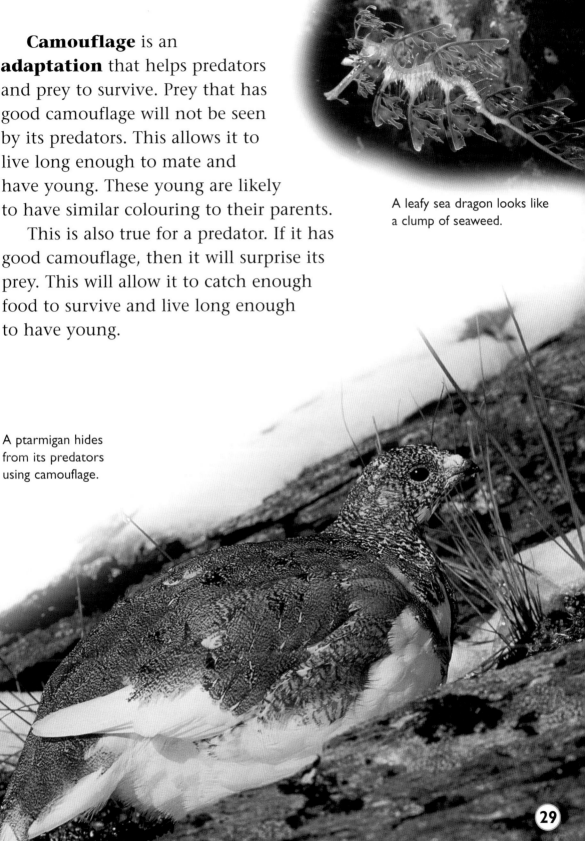

A ptarmigan hides from its predators using camouflage.

What's Next?

Many plant and animal **species** that once lived on Earth are now **extinct**. Many of them disappeared when they could not adapt to their changing environment. However, **adaptation** isn't something that happened only in the past. It continues all the time.

Today people are building and using land, which is home to many plants and animals. This means that the animals have to adapt or move on. If they don't adapt to their new surroundings, then they will not survive.

People in many countries are working hard to save plants and animals in danger of extinction. However, only time will tell what will happen next.

Both the tiger and the leatherback turtle are threatened by extinction today.

Glossary

adaptation — a feature of a plant or animal species that makes it more able to survive

behavioural adaptation — an adaptation that involves the way an animal behaves

camouflage — the way an animal's colour, pattern or shape disguises its presence

concealing colouration — colouring that helps an animal blend in with its surroundings

disguise — camouflage that makes an animal look like a certain object such as a flower

disruptive colouration — colour patterns that break up an animal's outline, making it hard to pick out one from a group or background

extinction — complete disappearance of a species

migration — seasonal movement of a large number of animals

mimicry — camouflage that makes an animal look like another animal; behavioural adaptation that allows animals to imitate actions like "playing dead"

species — a group of plants or animals that are alike in many ways and produce offspring together

Index